THANK YOU FOR CHOOSING MY BOOK.

Note : {xx} : Hit the notes in parentheses together

Tank Drump Notes

Thank you very much for choosing me. I hope you enjoyed. waiting for your positive feedback

SONGS

Endless Love

{1*6*}13 76{75*}7* 3

{64*}6*1 54{31} {25*}

{16*}23 {7*5*} 3 {6*4*}4* {7*5*}5*

{6*3*} 3 {7*5*} {6*4*}7*1 2{31}

{6*4*} 6 {55*}7* 65 2{31} 13

{6*4*} 6 {55*}7* 234 {36*}{25*}{16*}

{6*4*} 3 {25*} 7*{6*3*} 3*7*13 3*

{6*3*} 3 {7*5*} 5{6*4*}12 1{31}

5*{64*}4* 6{55*}7* 65

2{44*} 13 2{31}

5*{64*}4* 6{55*}7* 234

{36*}1 {25*}7* {16*}6*   {6*4*}4* 3 {25*}5* 7*{6*3*} 7*123

67{1*6} 2*3*1* {75*}7* 5   {64*}1*2* 3*{3*1}3

67{1*6} 2*3*1* {75*}7* 5   {64*}1*2* 1*{1*6*}1

67{1*6} 2*3*1* {75*}7* 5   {64*}1*2* 3*{3*1}3

67{1*6} 2*3*1* {75*}7* 5   {64*}1*2* 1*{1*6*}1

67{1*6}1 2*3*1* {75*}7*2 5   {64}6* 1*2* 3*{3*1}3

67{1*6}1 2*3*1* {75*}7*2 5   {64*}6* 1*2* 1*{1*6*}1

67{1*6}1 2*3*1* {75*}7*2 5   {3*1}2* 1*2* 1*2* {3*1}3

67{1*6}1 2*3*1* {75*}7*2 5   {3*1}2* 1*2* 1*{16*}1

67{1*6}1 2*3*1* {75*}7*2 5   {64}6* 1*2* 3*{3*1}3

67{1*6}1 2*3*1* {75*}7*2 5   {64*}6* 1*2* 1*{1*6*} 1316*

{1*6*}2*3*1* {75*}7* 5   5 {64*} 6*131*

{75*} 7*252*   6 5 {66*} 131 {6*3**}

3

Speechless

{6*3**}12 6{36*}1 6{31} 3**

{6*3**}12 6{36*}1 6{31} 3**

{6*3**}124 321{7*5*} 12{16*}

{6*4*} 7*1{7*5*} 12{27*}5* {16*}

{6*3**}124 321{7*5*} 12{16*}

{6*4*} 7*15 31{36*}1 {27*}7*2 135 {6*4*}6*13

5 {6*4*}6*15 3{25*}7*25 5*7*2

3 5 3{6*4*}6*13

5 {6*4*}6*5 361*{7*5*}7*22* 5*7*2

1*1* 7{6*4*}6*13*

{2*5*}7* 3*2*1* {55*}7*2 2*

1* {2*5*}7* 1*76 {36*}131*

4

1*7{64*}6* 1*7{66*}1   1*7 {66*}13 {6*3**} 1*

1* 7{6*4*}6*1 3*   {2*5*}7* 3*2*1* {55*}7*2 2*

1* {2*5*}7* 1*76 {36*}13 1*   1*7{64*}6* 1*7{66*}1

1*7 {66*}13 {6*3**}   17* {6*4*}4* 6*7*1{7*5*}5*

12{36*}1 43 1{6*4*}   17* {6*4*}4* 6*7*15

31 {36*}1 {25*}7*2   12 {46*}1 43 4{31}

1*1* 7{6*4*}6*1 3*   {2*5*}7* 3*2*1* {55*}7*2 2*

1* {2*5*}7* 1*76 {36*}13 1*   1*7{64*}6* 1*7{66*}1

1*7 {66*}13 {6*3**}   1*1* 7{6*4*}6*1 3*

{2*5*}7* 3*2*1* {55*}7*2 2*   1* {2*5*}7* 1*76 {36*}13 1*

1*7{64*}6* 1*7{66*}1   1*7 {66*}13 {6*3**}

5

Perfect

5*6* 1{15*}5*1

123 {25*} 7 5*

123 {44*}6*13 {24*}

5 55 6 32 {31}3 {31}

321 {44*}6*13 {24*}

321{31}3 {31}

321 {44*}6*13 {24*}

{1*6*}1 76 7{31}1

{1*4*}1 76 7{36*}1

35 {1*4*}6* 76 7{36*}

{25*}7* {44*}6*13

1 1 {31} {27*} {16*}

3 21 {36*} 6*1 12 3{34*}6*1 6*

3 21 {31} 13 5 3{26*}6*1 6*

123 {25*} 5*7*25

321 {36*}13 {31}

5* {31}1 43{25*}5*

321{36*}13 {31}

5* {25*} 7* 5* 3 2{16*}6*

{55*}7* 43 4{36*}1

{55*}7* 55 6{36*}21

123 {55*}7* 43 4{36*}1

12{36*}1 {25*}5* 2

{7*5*} {6*4*} {7*5*} {15*}

BELLA CIAO

3** 6*7*{16*}6* 3**

3** 6*7*{16*}6* 7*6*{1*6*}6* 7*6*

3 2 3 {44*}6*1 6*

1{7*5*}5* 3{7*5*}51{6*3**}

3** 6*7*{16*}6* 3**

7*6* {36*}1{36*}1{36*}

432 {46*}13 6*

3 2 3 {44*}6*1 6*

1{7*5*}5* 3{7*5*}51{6*3**} 3**6*

3** 6*7*{16*}6* 3**

7*6* {36*}1{36*}1{36*}

1{7*5*}5* 3{7*5*}51{6*3**} 3**6*

3** 6*7*{16*}6* 3**

{36*}1{36*}1{36*}

432 {46*}13 6*

3**6* 3** 6*7*{16*}6* 3**

3** 6*7*{16*}6* 7*6*{1*6*}6*

3 2 3 {44*}6*1 6*

1{7*5*}5* 3{7*5*}51{6*3**} 3**6*

654 {66*}13 6*

3** 6*7*{16*}6* 3**

3** 6*7*{16*}6* 7*6*{1*6*}6*

3 2 3 {44*}6*1 6* 432 {46*}13 6*

1{7*5*}5* 3{7*5*}51{6*3**} 3**6*

Himawari No Yakusoku

{31}21 {27*} {46*}13 2{31}

23{44*} 6*1 1*

23 {44*}6* 32{31}

17* {14*} 23{25*}5*

23 {44*}6* 32{31}

23 {44*}6* 321{7*5*} 12{15*}5*1

{25*}17* 1 {54*}6*1 65

3{36*}1 221 {6*4*}1

{1*6*}1 76{55*} 7*

{31}21 {27*}5*

21 {16*} 23 {25*}5*

{31}21 {27*}5*

21 {1*6*}1 76{55*} 7*

6{54*}6*1 2{31}

{54*}6*1 43{25*}7*5*

{54*}6* 434 5{64*}6*1 5

53 2 {16*}6*

1 {54*}6* 43 4{46*}1

6* {36*} 21 2{25*}

{54*}6* 434 5{64*}6*1 5

53 2 {16*}6*

1 {1*6*}11*1* 5{54*}6* 44

6 {44*}6* 32 1{16*}

1{31}11 7*{15*} 5*1

{1*6*}1 76{55*}7*

{36*}1 212 23{44*}6*

1{25*} 171 {64*}6*1 5

6 {44*}6* 32 3{31}

6 {1*6}6 2 2{2*5*}5

{36*}1 212 23{44*}6*

1{25*} 171 {64*}6*1 5

1 {55*}7* 32 3{25*}7* 11

16*1 {25*}7*5*

{31}21 {27*} {46*}13 2{31}

23{44*}6*1 321{7*5*} 12{15*}

Fly Me To The Moon

{1*6*}13 765 {44*}6*1

561* {75*}7*2 654 {36*}136*

{64*}6*1 543 {25*}7*2

346 {55*}7*2 432 {16*}6*1

1{14*}6*1 66 6*1

1*7{55*}7*2 5*7*2

6{64*}4*6* 44 6*1

654{36*}13 {7*5*}5*

{1*6*}13 765 {44*}6*1

561* {75*}7*2 654 {36*}136*

{64*}6*1 543 {25*}7*2

346 {55*}7*2 432 {16*}6*1

1{14*}6*1 66 6*1

1*7{3*6*}13 6*13

3* {3*4*}6*11*1* 4*6*1

17*{16*}131 {6*3**}

LA VIE EN ROSE

{1*6*}13 765 3 1*{75*}7*2   6531 7 {64*}6*1

5431 7 {64*}6*135 1

{2*5*}7*2 1*764 1*{75*}7*2

6542 7 {64*}6*1

5431 7 {64*}6*135 1

{1*6*}13 765 3 1*{75*}7*2   6531 7 {64*}6*1

5431 6 {64*}6*135 1   {2*5*}7*2 1*2*2*

1*{2*5*}7*2 1*5 5*   {2*5*}7*2 1*2*2*

1*{2*5*}7*2 3*1*2* 5

{1*6*}13 765 3 1*{75*}7*2

6531 7 {64*}6*1   5671* 2* {1*6*}135 1*

11

Stay With Me

{16*}1 3{64*}6*6 7{55*}7*5

{16*}1 3{64*}6*6 7{55*}7*5 3

12 {31} 3 3 {44*}6*1

12 {31} 3 5 {44*}6*

1*7{55*}7*5 6{55*}7*2

765 {31}1 3 {25*}5*

765 {31}1 3 {25*}5*

5*{16*}11 1 {16*}6*

5*{16*}1 2{31} 212 {16*} {7*5*}3**

5*{16*}11 1 {16*}6*

5*{16*}1 2{31} 212 {16*} {7*5*}3**

3{55*}7*5 2

34{55*}7*5 43 {25*}5*

3 {1*6*}13 35 {64*}6*

3 {1*6*}13 35 {64*}6*

17* {16*} {6*3**}

5*{16*}11 1 {14*}6*

5*{16*}11 1 {14*}6*

{36*}1 5{16*}

345 {44*}6* 321

{55*}7* 43 21

{36*}1 5{16*}

1345 {44*}6*

321 {31}

12 {31} 3 3 {44*}6*1

34{55*}7*5 43 {25*}5*

12 {31} 3 5 {44*}6*

1*7{55*}7*5 6{55*}7*2

3 {1*6*}13 35 {64*}6*

765 {31}1 3 {25*}5*

3 {1*6*}13 35 {64*}6*

765 {31}1 3 {25*}5*

17* {16*} {6*3**}

{16*}1 3{64*}6*6 7{55*}7*5

3{55*}7*5 2

{16*}1 3{64*}6*6 7{55*}7*53

FADED

{16[*]}11 3{64[*]}6[*] 66

5{31}33 3 {7[*]5[*]}7[*]7[*] 6[*]

{16[*]}11 3{64[*]}6[*] 66

5{31}33 3 {7[*]5[*]}7[*]7[*] 6[*]

{16[*]}11 6[*]16[*]1 2{31} 115[*] 3

111 {7[*]5[*]}5 7[*]7[*] 6[*]

{16[*]}11 6[*]16[*]1 2{31} 115[*] 3

11 2{27[*]}5[*] 333{31}

11 3{64[*]}6[*] 66

5{31}33 3 {7[*]5[*]}7[*]7[*]

333{31} 11 12{27[*]}11

333{31} 11 12{7[*]5[*]}7[*]7[*] 1

333{31} 11 3{64[*]}6[*] 66

1 5{31}1 1 55{31}{27[*]}

333{31} 11 116[*]{44[*]}6[*]1

5{31}53 5{31}

222{44[*]}6[*]1 6[*]4 3

{16[*]}11 1 1[*]7{64[*]}6[*] 66

5{31}33 3 {7[*]5[*]}7[*]7[*] 6[*]

{16[*]}11 1 1[*]7{64[*]}6[*] 66

5{31}3 5431{7[*]5[*]}5[*] 1 4 3

{16[*]}11 3{64[*]}6[*] 66

5{31}33 3 {7[*]5[*]}7[*]7[*] 6[*]

{16[*]}11 3{64[*]}6[*] 66

5{31}33 3 {7[*]5[*]}7[*]7[*]

STILL

1[*] 75{31}1 1[*] 75{27[*]}7[*]

56 7{75[*]}7[*]2 2[*]{64[*]}6[*]1

{31}1 5 7[*] {16[*]}6[*]7[*]1

1{64[*]}6[*]1 2 1{25[*]}7[*]5[*]

{31}1 5 7[*] {16[*]}6[*]7[*]1

1{44[*]}6[*] 3{27[*]}5[*] 1{25[*]}5[*]7[*]25

351[*]7{64[*]}6[*] 661 55 5[*]7[*]

351[*]7{64[*]}6[*] 6

{75[*]}7[*]2 1[*]{1[*]6[*]}136[*]

351[*]7{64[*]}6[*] 661 55 5[*]7[*]

345 {16[*]} 3{25[*]}5[*] 1{15[*]} 5[*]1

{31}1 5 7[*] {16[*]}6[*]7[*]1

1{64[*]}6[*]1 2 1{25[*]}7[*]5[*]

{31}1 5 7[*] {16[*]}6[*]7[*]1

1{44*}6* 3{27*}5* 1{25*} 5*7*25

351*7{64*}6* 661 55 5*7*

351*7{64*}6* 6

{75*}7*2 1*{1*6*}136*

351*7{64*}6* 661 55 5*7*

345 {16*} 3{25*}5* 1{15*} 5*1

351*7{64*}6* 661 55 5*7*

351*7{64*}6* 6

{75*}7*2 1*{1*6*}136*

351*7{64*}6* 661 55 5*7*

345 {16*} 3{25*}5* 1{15*} 5*

345 {16*} 3{25*}5* 1{15*} 5*1

16

Greensleeves

6{16*} 2{36*}1 43{25*} 7*{5*3**}

6*7*{14*} 6*{6*4*} 5*6*{7*5*} 5*3***

6{16*} 2{36*}1 43{25*} 7*{5*3**}

6*7*{14*}6* 7*6*{5*3***} 3***5*{6*3**}

6* {6*3***} 7*123 {51}5* 5{55*}7*

43{25*} 7*{5*3**}

6*7*{14*} 6*{6*4*} 5*6*{7*5*} 5*3** 5*

{54*}6*15 43{25*} 7*{5*3**}

6*7*{14*}6* 7*6*{5*3***}3***5*{6*3**} 6*{6*3**}

6{16*} 2{36*}1 43{25*} 7*{5*3**}

6*7*{14*} 6*{6*4*} 5*6*{7*5*} 5*3**

6{16*} 2{36*}1 43{25*} 7*{5*3**}

6*7*{14*}6* 7*6*{5*3**} 3**5*{6*3**}

6* {6*3**} 7*123 {51}5* 5{55*}7*

43{25*} 7*{5*3**}

6*7*{14*} 6*{6*4*} 5*6*{7*5*} 5*3** 5*

{54*}6*1 5 43{25*} 7*{5*3**}

6*7*{14*}6* 7*6*{5*3**} 3**5*{6*3**} {6*3**}

18

The Lord of The Rings Medley

{6*3**}5* 5*5*{6*3**}3**

23{44*}6*1 32{16*}

23{25*}5* {16*} {7*5*} {6*3*}

5* 3***5*{6*3**}3**

23{44*}6*1 32{16*}

23{36*}13 16*1{15*}5*3***

12{31}53 2{31} 21 5*

35{64*}6*1 3

1*75{31}6* 43{25*}5*

12{31}53 2{16*} 21 6*

35{64*}6*1

5 3{36*}1 {25*}5*

12{31}53 2{31} 21 5*

35{64*}6*1 3

1*75{31}6* 43{25*}5*

12{31}53 2{16*} 6*

35{64*}6*1

5 3{36*}1 {25*}5*

12{31}1 367 {1*4*}6*1

{75*}7*2 5{36*}1 43{25*}5*

12{31}1 34{54*}6*1 21{15*}5*1

12{31}53 2{16*} 6* 35{64*}6*1 3

1*75{31}6* 43{25*}5*

12{31}53 2{16*} 6* 35{64*}6*1

5 3{36*}1 {25*}5* 12{31}1 367 {1*4*}6*1

{75*}7*2 5{36*}1 43{25*}5*

12{31}1 367 {1*4*}6*1

{2*5*}7*2 {3*1}31 1*6*1*{15*}5*1

{6*3**}5* 5*5*{6*3**}3** 23{44*}6*1 32{16*}

23{25*}5* {16*} {7*5*} {6*3*} 5*3**5*{6*3**}3**

23{44*}6*1 32{16*}

23{36*}13 16*1{15*}5*1

Leaving On A Jetplane

{16*} 6*31{44*}6*13 2

1{5*3**}3** 5*

12{44*}6* 31 5*5*{6*4*}12

{46*}1 31 5*{6*4*}121

{44*}6* 321

{46*}1 32 1{25*}7*5*

12{44*}6* 31 5*5*{6*4*}121

{46*}1 31 5*{6*4*}121

{46*}1 32 1{25*}7*2

5{51}5* 35 {44*}6* 31 6*5*

5{31}5 {44*}6* 31 6*5*

5{31}5 {44*}6*

32 1{25*}7*2

5{51}5* 3

{64*}6* 5 4 5 5*

5{31}5 {44*}6* 54 3{16*}5*

65 {44*}6* 3 2 1{5*3**} 3** 5*

{46*}1 31 5*{6*4*} 1 2 1

{46*}1 32 1{25*} 7*5*

{46*}1 31 5*{6*4*} 1 2 1

{46*}1 32 1{25*} 7*2

5{31}5 {44*}6* 31 6*5*

32 1{25*}7*2

5 {44*}6* 3 2 1{25*} 7* 2

{64*}6* 5 4 5 5*

5 {44*}6* 3 2 1{5*3**}

12{44*}6* 31 5*5*{6*4*} 12

{44*}6* 3 2 1

12{44*}6* 31 5*5*{6*4*} 1 2 1

{44*}6* 3 2 1

5{51}5* 35 {44*}6* 31 6*5*

5{31}5 {44*}6*

5{51}5* 3 {64*}6* 5 4 5 5*

5{51}5* 3

5{31}5 {44*}6* 54 3{16*}5*

My Valentine

{15*} 5*7*12 {16*}

6*7* {14*}6* 2

7*12 {6*4*}4*

5*7*12 {16*}

6*{6*4*} 5*6*7*

{54*}6*1 43 2 {51}

{54*}6*1 43 2 {16*}6*

3 {14*}6* 3

6*{5*3**} 33 3{44*}6*

5*7*12 {16*}

5*7*12 {31}6* 11

{15*} 5*7*12 {16*}

6*{6*4*} 5*5* 4*{5*3**}

7*12 {31}6* 11

{55*}7*25 6

55 {55*}7*2 6

12{36*} 43 {25*}5*

{64*}6* 5 {16*}6*

11 7*{15*}

5*7*12 {31}6* 11　　6*7* {14*}6* 2

{15*} 5*7*12 {16*}　　7*12 {6*4*}4*

6*{6*4*} 5*5* 4*{5*3**}　　5*7*12 {16*}

7*12 {31}6* 11　　6*{6*4*} 5*6*7*

{55*}7*25 6　　{54*}6*1 43 2 {51}

55 {55*}7*2 6　　{54*}6*1 43 2 {16*}6*

12{36*} 43 {25*}5*　　3 {14*}6* 3

{64*}6* 5 {16*}6*　　6*{5*3**} 33 5{44*}6*

11 7*{15*}　　5*7*12 {16*}

5*7*12 {31}6* 11　　6*7* {14*}6* 2

Let It Go Ost Frozen

{31}4 6*34 {46*}3 6*43

{27*}3 5*23 5* 1{7*5*}{6*4*}

{31}4 6*34 {46*}3 6*43

{27*}3 5*23 5* 1{7*5*}{6*4*}

{36*}133 3{31} 211

11{25*}7*2 17*{6*4*} 4*

{36*}133 5{54*}6*1 3

11{25*}7*2 21{27*} 7*5*{16*}

33 5 {54*} 6* 53 5

{55}7* 5 434{31}16*4*

3321{25*}7* 3321{6*4*}

5* {6*4*}5* 6* 7* {15*}

5*5* 1{15*} 5*5* 1{25*}7*

21 21 {25*}7* 34 3{31}

5*5* 1{15*} 5*5* 1{25*} 7* 27*2

123 {44*} 6*1 3

67 {1*6*}13 55 {2*7*}7*2

1 {6*4*}66* 67{16*}13

67 {1*6*}13 63*{2*5*}7*2

1*2* {31}3***3 2*{16*}16*

{55*}7* 3{27*}

11 {54*}6*3 {16*}

11{7*5*}1 {54*}6*135

{44*}6* 43 43 43{16*}

25

Let Her Go (Passenger)

2321 {6*4*}1 6*{31} 6*

2321 {6*4*}1 6*

2321 {6*4*}1 6*{31} 6*

2321 {6*4*}1 6*

2321{14*}6* 16*16*1 6*

2321{24*}6* 16*6* 5*{15}

2321{14*}6* 16*16*1 6*

2321{24*}6* 16*6* 5*{15}

{6*3***} 6* {6*4*} 6* {7*5*}5* 12 5*

{6*4*} 6* {6*4*} 6* {7*5*}5* 12 5*

{36*}13 3221{14*}6*

2321 {6*4*}1 6*3{25*}5*

{54*}6* 3 12{36*}1 3 6*

2321 {6*4*}1 6*3{25*}5*

{54*}6* 3 12{36*}1 3 6*

2321{25*}7* 213 2{16*}6*

5*{27*} 7* 2

2321{25*}7* 213 2{16*}6*

5*{27*} 7* 2 21 321

43 {31}6* 2 217*{7*5*}

26

5* 32 {16*}6* 3 2{14*}6*   5*{27*} 7* 2 5*

{36*}13 3221{14*}6*   43 {31}6* 2 217*{7*5*}

5* 32 {16*}6* 3 2{14*}6*   5*{27*} 7* 2 5*

2321{14*}6* 16*16*1 6*

2321{25*}7* 213 2{16*}6*

2321{24*}6* 16*6* 5*{15*}   5*{27*} 7* 2

2321{14*}6* 16*16*1 6*

2321{25*}7* 213 2{16*}6*

2321{24*}6* 16*6* 5*{15*}

5*{27*} 7* 2 21 321 {15*}

Stay With Me
(Miki Matsubara)

{6*4*} 6*6* 7*17*12

{6*4*} 6*6* 7*17*12

{27*}3*5* 3*5*7* 3*5*7*

{6*4*} 6*6* 7*17*12

{6*4*} 6*6* 7*17*12

{27*}3*5* 3*5*7* 3*5*7*

{6*4*} 22 3{46*} 323

{25*}5*1 6*1{36*} 212 {31}

6*1{36*} 21 3{25*} 5*7*5*

{6*4*} 22 3{46*} 323 {25*}5*1

6*1{36*} 212 {31}

6*1{36*} 21 3{25*} 5*7*2 5

12 {36*} 1 1{31}33

22 5 44 {46*}13 6*136*

1{36*} 1 1{31}33

22 {46*}1 33{34*}6*1 4*6*14*

6*1{31} 45{16*}

6*1{31} 45{16*}

2{15*} 5*{15*} 2{36*}13 6*

{36*}143 2{36*}13 6*

{36*}143 2{36*}13 6*

{36*}143 2{36*}13 1{6*3**}

Photograph

3** 17*1 5*4*3**   3** 17*1 5*4*3**

3** 17*1 5*4*3**   3** 17*1 5*4*3**

332 {31} 11 5*1   332 {31} 11 6*1

112 {7*5*}5*1   1 {44*}6* 32

1 {14*}6*3 4* 6*   332 {31} 11 5*1

332 {31} 11 6*1   112 {7*5*}5*1

2 {44*}6* 32   1 {14*}6*3 4*6*14*

{16*} 11111 1 {25*}7* 33

{6*4*} 11111 1 {25*}7* 33   12 {56*}1 3221

{55*}7* 3221   {54*}6* 322 11

{7*5*}5*7* 1{27*} 5*   112 {31} 5*

{31}334 321{36*}1 2 6*

30

{31}334 321{34*}6* 2 6*   {31}334 321{14*}6* 3

4*6*14*   112 {31} 5*   {31}334 321{36*}1 2 6*

{31}334 321{54*}6*13 6*   {31}334 321{16*} 6*1

{16*}1 7* 1{15*} 5*1   {16*}1 7* 1{16*} 6*1

{31}3 2 3{31} 13   {16*}1 7* 1{25*} 7*2 34

112 {31} 5*   {31}334 321{36*}1 2 6*

{31}334 321{34*}6* 2 6*   {31}334 321{14*}6* 3

4*6*14*   112 {31} 5*   {31}334 321{54*}6*13 6*

{31}334 321{36*}1 2 6*   {31}334 321{14*} 6*1

{31}334 321{14*} 6*1   {16*}1 7* 1{15*} 5*1

{16*}1 7* 1{5*3**} 3**5*   {16*}1 7* 1{15*} 5*{15*}

Shape Of You

{36*}33 {6*4*}6*6*

{14*}11 {25*}22

{36*}33 {6*4*}6*6*

{14*}11 {25*}22

{6*3**}16* {6*4*}16*

{6*4*}16* {7*5*}6*5*

{6*3**}16* {6*4*}16*

{6*4*}16* {7*5*}6*5*

{16*}11 {16*}11

{14*}6* 112 3{31}5*

{56*}133 2{25*}7*2

321 {25*}7*2 321 {6*4*}

6*{31}33 {36*}33

{36*} 3321 {31} 21

{56*}133 2{25*}7*2

321 {25*}7*2 321 {6*4*}

4*3**3** 5*6* 5*{6*3**}

6*6* 5*{6*4*} 32

{25*}7*21{6*4*} 1321 {6*4*}

53 {25*}16*

{25*}7*2 32 {16*} 21 {6*3**}

6*6* 5*{6*4*} 32

{25*}7*21{6*4*}1321{6*4*}

53{25*}16*

12{31}2112{25*}5*

12{31}2112{25*}5*

12{31}5321{25*}5*

12{31}6*12{25*}5*

{6*4*}6*11{25*}233{6*4*}

{6*4*}6*11{25*}233{6*4*}

{6*4*}6*11{25*}233{6*4*}

12{31}212{6*4*}

33212 3 6*6*3*** 33212 3 6*6*3***

{6*3***}16*{6*4*}16*

{6*3***}16*{6*4*}16*

53{25*}16*4*

{6*4*}{7*5*}3**5*6*{6*3***}

12{31}2112{6*4*}4*

12{31}2112{6*4*}4*

12{31}212{6*4*}4*

12{31}212

12{31}212

12{31}212

12{31}2112{25*}5*

{6*3***}33212 3 6*6*3***

33212 3 6*6*

{6*4*}16*{7*5*}6*5*

{6*4*}16*{7*5*}6*5*

Memories (Maroon 5)

{31} 13 1 {25*}7*2 7*{15}

{54*}6* 345 34{54*} 6*1　　　　　　{36*} 123 12{31}6*

21{6*4*}6*6* 6*5*{6*4*} 5*5* 3*　　{6*4*}4* 6*6* 1{7*5*} 5*

{54*}6* 345 34{54*} 6*1　　　　　　{36*} 123 12{31}6*

21{6*4*}6*6* 6*5*{6*4*} 5*5* 3*　　{6*4*}4* 6*6* 1{7*5*}

5* 7*7* 1{15}　　　　　　　　　　12{31} 55 3{64*}6*13

23{46*}1 54 3{16*} 6*　　　　　　23{44}6*14 3{36*}1 2

1{14*}6*1 34{25*} 5*　　　　　　12{31} 55 3{64*}6*13

23{46*}1 54 3{16*} 6*　　　　　　23{44}6*14 3{36*}1 2

11{14*}6*1 34{25*} 7*2　　　　　{16*}6* 1131 {14*}6* 1131

{7*5*}5*7* 1 4*　　　　　　　　{16*}6* 1131 {14*}6* 1151

34

{7*5*} 5*7*1

{54*}6* 345 34{54*} 6*1

{36*} 123 12{31}6*

21{6*4*}6*6* 6*5*{6*4*}5*5* 3*

{6*4*}4* 6*6* 1{7*5*}5*

{54*}6* 345 34{54*} 6*1 {36*} 123 12{31}6*

21{6*4*}6*6* 6*5*{6*4*}5*5* 3*

{6*4*}4* 6*6* 1{7*5*}

5* 7*7* 1{15}

5 3{25*}7* 2 1{6*4*}

5 {25*}7*2 {16*}

{16*}6* 1151 {14*}6* 11

{7*5*} 5*7* {15*}

Someone You Loved

{3*1}53*53*53*5

{75*}2 72 72 72

{1*6*}31*31*31*3

{64*}1 61 61 61

{5*3**}55 353 53

{65*}765 {54*}6

5 {31}2 4*6*14*

{5*3**}55 353 53

{65*}765 {54*}6

5 {31}2 4*6*14* {5*3**}

56 55 {3*1}3

565 3* {2*5*}7*

5555 {1*6*}13

3*3*2*1* {64*}6*1

56 55 {3*1}3

565 3* {2*5*}7*2 5*

3*3*3* {3*1}3 2*2*{2*5*}7*

1*1* {1*6*}1 2*1* 6*131

{64*}6*1 66 {64*}6* 55

3 {36*}1 22

23 {44*}6*1 321

{64*}6*1 66 {64*}6* 55

3 {36*}1 2 3 4   {6*4*} 111 443

{6*4*}4* 11 443   {14*}6* 11 443

{16*}6* 11 553 {7*5*}5*   11 443 {6*4*}4*

11 443 {14*} 6* 1

333 {36*}1 22{25*}7*

11{14*}6* 21 4*6*14*

{3*1}5 3*5 3*5 3*5   {75*}2 72 72 72

{1*6*}31*31*31*3   {64*}1 61 61 61

Despacito

{6*3**}3**6*7*1 217*

6*5*4*11{14*}

{15*}5* 15* 15* 12{25*}7* 5*

{6*3**}3**6*7*1 217*

6*5*4*11 2{1*4}

{15*}5* 15* 15* 12{25*}7* 5*

{36*} 2323 23 23 23

4{44*}6*11{41}6*4

5{46*}131 1{36*}13

4{36*} {25*}5*

{36*} 2323 23 23 23

4{44*}6*11{41}6*4

5{46*}131 1{36*}13

4{36*} {25*}5*

17* {6*3**}3** 3**{6*3**}6*

5* {6*4*}4* 4*{6*4*}6*

7* {15*}5* 5*{15*}1

2 {25*}7* 5*

17* {6*3**}3** 3**{6*3**}6*

5* {6*4*}4* 4*{6*4*}6*

7* {15*}5* 5*{15*}1

2 {25*}7* 5*

{36*} 2323 23 23 23   4{44*}6*1 1{41}6*4

5{46*}13 1{36*}13   4{36*} {25*} 5*

{36*} 2323 23 23 23   4{44*}6*1 1{41}6*4

5{46*}13 1{36*}13   4{36*} {25*} 5*

1 7* {6*3**}3** 3**{6*3**}6*

5* {6*4*}4* 4*{6*4*}6*

7* {15*}5* 5*{15*}1   2 {25*} 7* 5*

1* 7 {66*} 13 366   5 {64*}6*4 466

7 {1*5*}15 51*1*   2* {2*5*}7*7 5

1* 7 {66*} 13 366   5 {64*}6*4 466

7 {1*5*}15 51*1*   2* {2*5*}7*7 5

1* 7 {66*}

Take Me To Your Heart

{36*}1 23 2{31}1

1 {36*}1 23 2{31}{15*}

{15*}1 2 3{31}

5*6*1 6* {16*}1 2 3{16*} 6*

{14*}6*1 2 3{31}

6*16* {25*}7*2

3 6*{25*} 7*5* {16*}

11 2 {36*}1 5

{14*}6*1 2 3{31} {25*} {16*}

11 2 {36*}1 5

{36*}122 1{31}2

5*6*1 6* {16*} 123 2{31}

5*6*1 6*{14*}6* 123 {25*}

5*6*1 6* {16*} 123 2{31}

5*6*1 6*{14*}6* 12 6{55*}7*

3 5{51}3 56{1*6*}13 6

{54*}6*1 5 6{1*6*}13 6

561* 6 {1*6*}13

3 {36*}122 1{31} 2

65 {64*}6* 35

{31} 3 23 {25*} 5* {15*}

65 {64*}6* 35

3 {36*}122 1{31} 2

65 {64*}6* 35

{31} 3 23 {25*} 5* {15*}

{36*}122 1{31}2

3 {36*}1 22 6 {55*}7*

65 {64*}6* 35

561* 6 {1*6*}13

3 {36*}12

561* 6 {1*6*}13

561* 6 {1*6*}13

3 {36*}12

A Whole New World

{31} 24 31 {5*3**} 3**

{27*} 132 7* {25*}7*

{31} 24 31 {5*3**} 3**

{27*} 132 7* {25*}7*

346 {55*}7*2 {16*}

{31} 45 {74*}6*1 65

1 {36*}1 22 1 {25*}5*

346 {55*}7*2 4 3{36*}1

1 {75*}7*2 1* 5

53 2 {15*}5* {15*}

12{31} 24 31 {36*}1 {25*}7*

171 {6*4*} 121 {5*3**} 3**5*

12{31} 24 31 {36*}1 {25*}7*

171 {6*4*} 121 {36*}1

346 {55*}7*2 4 3{36*}1

1 {75*}7*2 1* 5

346 {55*}7*2 {16*}

{31} 45 {74*}6*1 65

1 {36*}1 22 3 {44*}6*1

{31} 24 31 {5*3**} 3**

12{31} 24 31 {36*}1 {25*}7*   {27*} 132 7* {25*}7*

171 {6*4*} 121 {5*3**} 3**5*   {31} 24 31 {5*3**} 3**

12{31} 24 31 {36*}1 {25*}7*   {27*} 132 7* {25*}7*

171 {6*4*} 121 {36*}1   346 {55*}7*2 {16*}

346 {55*}7*2 4 3{36*}1   {31} 45 {74*}6*1 65

1 {75*}7*21* 5   1 {36*}1 22 1 {25*} 5*

346 {55*}7*2 {16*}

346 {55*}7*2 4 3{36*}1

{31} 45 {74*}6*1 65   1 {75*}7*21* 5

1 {36*}1 22 3 {44*}6*1   53 2 {15*} 5* {15*}

Here I Am To Worship

3 {25*}7* 23

{31} 34 {25*}7*

{36*}1 34 {25*}7*

{31} 34 {25*}7*

{36*}1 34 {25*}7*

433 2 {31} 3

35 {14*}6*

433 2 {36*} 13

5 {44*}6* 31

3 {25*}7* 23

5 {44*}6* 31

5 {44*}6* 31 4*6*14

23 {44*}6*1 3{25*}7* 1

23 {14*} 6*16*

23 {44*}6*1 3{25*}7* 1

23 {14*} 6*13 {6*4*}

433 2 {25*}7*2   433 2 {36*} 13

44 33 2 {31} 3   433 2 {25*}7*2

35 {14*} 6*1   3 {25*}7* 23

1 {25*}7* 23   5 {44*}6* 31

5 {44*}6* 31   1 {25*}7* 23

4*6*14* {15*}

Sound Of Silence

6*6* 11 33 2   5*5* 7*7* 22 1

11 33 55 6 65   11 33 55 6 65

11 1 66 67 1*1*   1*76 55 65 3

11 15 7*16*   6*6* 11 3 12

5*5* 7*7* 2 7*1   11 33 55 6 65

11 33 55 6 65   11 1 66 67 1*1*

1*76 55 65 3   11 15 7*16*

Heal The World

5*6*1 5*12 123 45 32   5*6*1 5*12 43 2 65

5*6*1 5*12 123 45 32   5*6*1 5*12 43 2 65

11 6 61*7 5   56 56 123 5

3 33 22 6* 6*6* 5*5*   5*6*1 3 33 44

2 5 5 5 5 44   5 4 3 323

35 61*7 5   556 56 123 5

333 22 6*6* 5*6* 5*5*   5*6*1 3 33 44

2 5 5 5 5 44   5 4 3 323

35 61*7 5   556 56 123 5

333 22 34 3 21   333 22 34 3 21

46

HAVANA

1 33 116*   323 43 21 33 116*   323 43 21 33 116*

323 43 21 31   3217* 12 7*   3217* 16*

6 66 33 43 23   32 32 11   6 66 33 43 23

32 32 11   6 66 71*7 67   32 32 11

6 66 33 43 23   32 32 11

6 56 3*2* 1*2*7   55 55 563

32 32 137*   6 56 3*2* 1*2*7   55 55 563

32 32 17*   1 33 116*   323 43 21 33 116*

323 43 21 33 116*   323 43 21 31   3217* 12 7*

3217* 16*

Right Here Waiting

{15*}5* 5543 {25*}7*   2234 {36*}12 3

{44*}6* 32 17* {15*}   5*1 2 {25*}7* 3

321 {27*} {6*4*} 4*

6*7* {14*}6* 27* 5* 6* {5*3*}3*

5*1 2 {25*}7* 3   431 {27*} {6*4*} 4*

6*7* {14*}6* 27* 5* 1 {16*} 6*

123 {44*}6* 31 2 {6*4*} 4*

123 {44*}6* 31 6* {5*3*} 5*   5543 {25*}7*

2234 {36*}11 2   {31}1 21 7*6* {5*3**} 5*

5543 {25*}7*   2234 {36*}12 3

{44*}6* 32 17* {15*}

5*12 {31}3 43 5* {6*4*}4*   12 {16*} {5*3**}3**

5*12 {31}3 43 5* {6*4*}4*   11 5 {55*}7*2 5

{15*}5* 5543 {25*}7*   2234 {36*} 11 2

{31}1 21 7*6* {5*3**}5*   5543 {25*}7*

2234 {36*}12 3

{44*}6* 32 17* {15*}

How Far I'll Go

15*15*15*15*1 2 6*2 6*   2 1233 3 3333 217*6*

15*15*15*1 2 6* 2   1212 33 2 3333 11

6*5*6* 11 6*5*6* 11   6*5*6* 22 6*5*6* 22

11 33 211 33 234 1 7*   123 123 123 11 5 2

56 32 56 32   123 123 123 11 5 2

5* 56 32   234 11 5*5* 22 11

123 123 123 11 5 2   56 32 56 32

123 123 123 11 5 2   5* 56 32

5*5* 55

I Want To Break Free

5*1 2 223

5*1 2 243

5*1 22 43 243 243

243 22 1   22 1 6*5*

3 2 43 143 11

5*1 2 223

5*1 22 43 243 243

243 22 1   22 1 6*5*

3 2 43 143 11

5* 7*7* 7*12 17*

22 22 32 1 1

123 2 11 123 6 321

44 43 211

11 17* 6*5*6*

44 43 211

5*1 2 223

5*1 22 43 243 243

243 221   22 1 6*5*

32 43 143 11

5*1 2 223

5*1 22 43 243 243

243 221

22 1 6*5*

32 43 143 11

Never Enough

{15*}5* 3{25*}7*

4{36*} 3**6*13 {15*}5* 3{25*}7*

5 4{36*} 3**6*16

{15*} 1123 {55*}1 2 {31} 13

13 {34*}6*1 {5*3**}

13 {34*}6*1 {7*5*}5* 7* 1{15*}

123{55*}1 6{36*}13

13 {34*}6*1 {5*3**}

13 {34*}6*2

{31} 24 4*6*1 1* 3 {64*}6*

1 65 1{36*}1

{34*}6* 3 4{31} {27*}

5*7*25* {15*}

111 5{55*}1 3321 {7*5*} 777

5{75*}7* 571*

{2*4*}6* 3*6 5{64*}6* 1*

{2*4*}6* 3*6 5{64*}6* 2*

1* {1*5*}1 55 3{31} 2211

1* {75*}7* 67 6{75*}7* 671*

{2*4*}6* 3*6 5{64*}6* 1*

{2*4*}6* 3*6 5{64*}6* 2*

1* {1*5*}1   {16*} 235 {31}2 32 {16*} 235 {31}2 32

{16*} 235 {31}2 32   {14*}6* 1 {14*}6* 2 {16*} 235 {31}2 32

{16*} 235 {31}2 32   {16*} 265 {31}2 32 {14*}6* 1 {14*}6* 2

{15*} 111 5{55*}1 3321   {7*5*} 777 5{75*}7* 571*

{2*4*}6* 3*6 5{64*}6* 1*   {2*4*}6* 3*6 5{64*}6* 2*

1* {1*5*}1 55 3{31} 2211   1* {75*}7* 67

6{75*}7* 671*   {2*4*}6* 3*6 5{64*}6* 1*

{2*4*}6* 3*6 5{64*}6* 2*   1* {1*5*}1

{16*} 235 {31}2 32

{16*} 235 {31}2 32 {16*} 235 {31}2 32

{14*}6* 1 {14*}6* 2

{16*} 235 {31}2 32 {16*} 235 {31}2 32

{16*} 265 {31}2 32   {14*}6* 1{44*} 6*136 3 {31}

Somebody That I Used to

11 22 345 32

11 7*7* 6*6* 5*

11 22 345 32

11 7*7* 6*6* 5*

3332 22 437* 6*7*6*

3332 225 32 13

3332 225 32

11 121 7*17* 6*6*

3332 222 437* 6*7*6*

6* 3 5 32 6*

6* 3 5 32 6*

332 225 32 67*6*

3332 224 3 7*6*5*5*

3332 225 32

11 121 7*17* 6*6*

3332 222 437* 6*76*

6*7*1 6*4 33

33 2222 5 5 5432 11   6*7*1 6*4 33

2 333 1 2222 11   6*7*1 6*4 33

33 2222 5 5 5432 11   6*7*1 6*4 33

2 333 1 2222 11   6* 3 5 32 6*

6* 3 5 32 6*

11 22 345 32

11 7*7* 6*6* 5*

11 22 345 32

11 7*7* 6*6* 5*

Thousand Years

3 3 3 2 3 3 3 2 4 4 4

1 3 2 17*5*

1 1 1 32 1 1 1 1

5 43 1 6* 5 43 2 3 7* 1

1 1 1 32 1 1 5 3

5 43 1 6* 5 43 2 3 7* 16*

6 7 1* 7

3 53 3 53 6 5 21

3 53 3 53 6 5 2

1234 3 6* 1234 3 2

3 53 3 53 6 5 21

3 53 3 53 6 5 2

1234 3 6* 1234 3 5*

1 2 3 2 6 7 1* 7

3 53 3 53 6 5 21

3 53 3 53 6 5 2

1234 3 6* 1234 3 2

3 53 3 53 6 5 21

3 53 3 53 6 5 2

1234 3 6* 1234 3 5*

Colors Of The Wind

{31} 55 3 {36*}

{27*} 33 4{44*}6* 32 1{27*}5*

221 {27*}5* {6*4*}5*

221 {36*} 13

221 {27*}5* {6*4*}

5*6*1{31} 55 3 {36*}1

{31} 55 3 {36*}1

1 {64*}6* 55 3{36*}1

13{25*}7* 123 {27*}5*

3 5 {1*6*}1 77 6{64*}6*

7{1*6*}1 77 6{64*}6*

{14*} 33 1 {16*}

{31} 55 3 {36*}1

{31} 55 3 {36*}1

1 {64*}6* 55 3{36*}1

13{25*}7* 123 5 23{6*3**}

221 {27*}5* {6*4*} 5*

221 {66*} 13 5

221 {27*}5* {6*4*}

16* 1{15*}

55 32{36*}1 5 6{64*}6*1

55 32 {31}13 5

57

3 5 {1*6*}1 77 6{64*}6*

6*13 {25*}7*

6*13 {25*}7*

3 5 {1*6*}1 77 6{64*}6*

7 {1*6*}1 77 6{64*}6*

3 5 {1*6*}1 77 6{64*}6*

6*13 {25*}7*

6*13 {25*}7*

55 6 {55*} 7* 2 3

1 {14*}4* 6* 1{25*}7*2

1 {14*}4*6* 1{15*}

55 32{36*}1 5 6{64*}6*1

55 32 {31}13 5

55 6 {55*}7* 2 3

1 {14*}4*6* 1{25*}7*2

1 {14*}4*6* 1{15*}

BAD LIAR

{15*}2 13 12 13 153   {15*}2 13 12 13 153

{15*}2 13 12 13 153   {15*}2 13 12 13 153

1{15*} 33 21{15*}5* 33   1{16*} 33 21{16*}6* 33

21 {6*4*} 1* 1*1* 7   {7*5*} 7 77 2* {1*5*}

13 15* 13   1{15*} 33 21{15*}5* 33

1{16*} 33 21{16*}6* 33   21 {6*4*} 1* 1*1* 7

{7*5*} 7 77 2* {1*5*}   13 15* 13

1*1*1* 7{66*}1   1*1*1* 7{51}5*

1*1*1* 7{1*6*} 13   1*1*1* 2*{2*5*}7*2

1*1*1* 7{64*}6*1   1*1*1* 7{55*}7*2

1*1*1* 7{1*6*} 13   1*1*1* 2*{2*5*}7*2 5*7*2

{15*} 1111 4{36*}

59

1 1 4{31}

1 1 2{25*}

1 1 4{31}

1 1 2{25*} 7*5*

{55*}7*2 321

12{31} 43{27*} 32{16*}6*

{15*} 1111 4{36*}

1 1 7*{14*}4*

1111 4{36*}

1 1 7*{14*}4*

{31}1 2 {44*}6*13

{31}1 2 {44*}6*1321

1 1 7*{14*}4*

1111 4{36*}

1 1 7*{14*}4*

{54*}6*1 321

1 {54*}6*1 32

1{14*}6* 11 2 {31} {27*}

1 1 4{31}

1 1 2{25*}

1 1 4{31}

1 1 2{25*}7*5*

21 {16*}6* 1{25*}7*5*

{16*}6* 1{25*}7*5*

Titanium (SIA)

55 61*7 55 2* 1*7 77 61*

55 61*7 55 63

55 61*7 55 2* 1*7 77 61*

55 61*7 55 63

6* 443 7*7* 33 7* 7*3 7* 16*

443 7*7* 66 7* 7* 7*3 7* 16*

665 33 55 333 1* 7 6

1 665 33 55 333 1* 7 6

665 33 55 333 1* 7 6

1 665 33 55 333 1* 7 6

5*5* 6*17* 5*5* 2 17* 7*7* 6*1

5*5* 6*17* 5*5* 6*3**

5*5* 6*17* 5*5* 2 17* 7*7* 6*1

5*5* 6*17* 5*5* 6*3**

6* 443 7*7* 33 7* 7*3 7* 16*

443 7*7* 66 7* 7* 7*3 7* 16*

665 33 55 333 1* 7 6

1 665 33 55 333 1* 7 6

665 33 55 333 1* 7 6

1 665 33 55 333 1* 7 6

A Time For Us (Romeo and Juliet)

61* 7 {36*}13

65 4 {55*}15*

321 2 {36*}13

35 3 {64*}6*136

5 {1*6*}13 765

1 {35*}5* 1 {25*}7*

1 {25*}7* 7* {14*}6*

61* 7 {36*}1316*

65 4 {55*}1315*

321 2 {36*}1316*

35 3 {64*}6*136

35 3 {64*}6*1

54 3 {25*}7*5*

61* 7 {36*}13

6 {2*5*}7* {75*}7*5*

{1*6*}1 76 5 {66*} 1 3 6*

23 {44*}6*1 2{36*}1

6* {7*5*} 5* 3** {6*3**}

35 3 {64*}6*16*4*

54 3 {25*}7*27*5*

61* 7 {36*}1316*

6 {2*5*}7*2 {75*}7*27*5*

5 {1*6*}13 765

{1*6*}1 76 5 {66*} 1316*   1 {35*}13 1 {25*}7*2

23 {44*}6*16* 2{36*}13

1 {25*}7*2 7* {14*}6*1

6* {7*5*}5*7* 5* 3** {6*3**}

61* 7 {36*}1316*   35 3 {64*}6*16*4*

65 4 {55*}1315*   54 3 {25*}7*27*5*

321 2 {36*}1316*   61* 7 {36*}1316*

35 3 {64*}6*136   6 {2*5*}7*2 {75*}7*27*5*

5 {1*6*}13 765   {1*6*}1 76 5 {66*}

131{6*3**}

64

Lily (Alan Walker)

3 2323 6 4

12 12 12 53 236* 6*6* 32 17*

3 2323 6 4

43217* 7*12 53 32 12 6* 13

2 46 7 71* 76

1* 65 1* 65 1* 71* 2*3**3** 2*1* 2* 6

1* 65 1* 65 1* 71*

2*3**3** 2*1* 2* 6 3 2323 6 4

43217* 7*12 53

32 12 6* 6*5*6* 32 17* 7*1 7*6*

33 66 4 44 321

22 55 3 43 212 6* 13

2 46 7 71* 76

1* 65 1* 65 1* 71* 2*3**3** 2*1* 2* 6

1* 65 1* 65 1* 71*

2*3**3** 2*1* 2* 6 3 2323 6 4

43217* 7*12 53

32 12 6* 6*6* 32 17* 7*1 7*6*

Davy Jones Theme Song
(Pirates of the Caribbean)

6* 7*1 23 543

3 45 543 23

4 53 12 431

6*7* 5*3*** 7*6* 1 3 6*

{6*3***} 7*{16*} 2{31} 54{31} 1

{36*}1 4{55*}7* 54{31} 2{31}1

{44*}6* 5{31} 1{25*}7* 43{16*}

6*{7*5*} 5*3*** 7*{6*3***}1 3 6*

{6*3***} 7*1 7*6* 7*1

{6*3***}3*** 7*{16*}6* 2{36*}1

54{36*}13

{36*}1 4{55*}7* 54{36*}1

2{36*}13

{44*}6* 5{31}6*1

{25*}7* 43{14*}4*

6*{7*5*}7*5* 3** 7**{6*3**} 1 3 6

{6*3**}3** 7*{16*}6* 2{36*}1

54{36*}13

{36*}1 4{55*}7* 54{36*}1

2{36*}13

{44*}6* 5{31}6*1

{25*}7* 43{14*}4*

6*{7*5*}7*5* 3** 7**{6*3**} 1 3 {6*3**}

Love of My Life (Queen)

{15*} 7* 15 1 {7*5*}{6*4*}   6* {46*}13 46

6* {5*3**} 55 4   {36*}1 216 5

6 {6*4} 6*136   43 {44*}6*1 42 {36*}13

3 {44*}6* 3 22   1 6*5*4* {16*}6* 4

6 {55*}7*2   {25*}7* 12 3 {44*}6*16*4*

{44*}6*1 4 4{36*}1 63   1{25*}7* 12 12

41 {6*4*}4* {5*3**}   {44*}6*1 4 4{36*}1 63

21 {36*}1 213   21 {7*5*}5* 55

5 {55*} 7*257   {15*} 7*15 1 {7*5*}{6*4*}

6* {46*}13 46

6* {5*3**} 55 4

{36*}1 216 5

6 {6*4} 6*136

43 {44*}6*1 42 {36*}13

3 {44*}6* 3 22

1 6*5*4* {16*}6* 4

6 {55*}7*27*5

{27*}12 3 {44*}6*134

All of Me

3 3 3 4 4 4 3 3 3 2 2 2

323 3 3 3211

1 323 3 3232 11 6*

33 4 31 4 31 2 32 6*

323 3 3 3211

333 543 32 11 6*

33 4 31 14 31 12 32 4

1 6 5 4 3 2 1 7* 6* 5*6*

6 6 543 3 212

35 36 3 2 13

33 2 22 12 6

33 2 22 12 5*

33 5 36 3 1*76 53

33 2 22 12 6

33 2 22 12 5*

33 451* 7 6 5 33

33 451* 7 6 5 33 32

35 36 3 2 13

33 2 22 12 6*

33 2 22 12 5*

33 5 36 3 1*76 53

33 2 22 12 6*

33 2 22 12 5*

33 451* 7 6 5 33

33 451* 7 6 5 33 32

GIVE THANKS

3{31}5* 21{25*} 7*5*

2{16*}6* 7*6*{7*5*} 5*3**

7*{6*4*}4* 7*16*{5*3**} 113

{27*}5* 1{25*}7*

3{31}5* 21{25*} 7*5*

2{16*}6* 7*6*{7*5*} 5*3**

7*{6*4*}4* 7*16*{5*3**} 113

{27*}5* 1{25*}7*

5{51}5* 55{54*}6*12

3{46*} 13

44{44*}6*7* 12{36*}1

33{34*} 6*7*

1{27*}5* 1{25*}7*

5{51}5* 55{54*}6*1 2 3

{56*} 434 6*

44{44*}6*7* 12{36*}1

33{34*} 6*7*

1{27*}5* 1{25*}7* 1{15*}

3{31}5*1 21{25*}5*7*5*

52{16*}6*1 7*6*{7*5*}7*5*3**

3***7*{6*4*}4*6* 7*16*{5*3***}3**

13 {25*}5*7* 1{27*}7*2   3{31}5*1 21{25*}5*7*5*

52{16*}6*1 7*6*{7*5*}7*5*3**

3***7*{6*4*}4*6* 7*16*{5*3***}3**

13 {25*}5*7* 1{27*}7*2

5{55*}72 55{54*}6*12   3{46*} 13

44{44*}6*7* 12{36*}13   33{34*} 6*7*

1{25*}5*7* 1{27*}7*2   5{55*}72 55{54*}6*12

3 {56*} 434 6*   44{44*}6*7* 12{36*}13

33{34*} 6*7*   1{25*}5*7* 1{27*}7*2 1{15*}

CARUSO

2321{7*5*}5* 6*{16*} 6*

7*{27*} 3{7*5*}

1{6*4*}4* {7*5*}5* 1{7*5*}

17*6*7*{16*} 217*1{27*}

3{7*5*} 1{6*4*}4*

{7*5*} {6*3**}

333{31} 6*13{54*}6*

43{27*} 7*5* {25*}

222{27*} 5*7*2{46*}1

3{14*} 6* {6*3**}

333{31} 6*13{54*}6*

43{27*} 7*5* {25*}

222{27*} 5*7*2{46*}1

3{14*} 6* {6*3**}

3 6 1*{1*4*}6*1

6*{46*}1 7*{25*}

777{75*}7*

2*1* {76*}1 6{36*}1 {6*3**}

3 6 1*{1*4*}6*1

6*{46*}1 7*{25*}

777{75*}7*

2*1* {76*}1 6{36*}1 {6*3**}

333{31} 6*13{54*}6*

43{27*} 7*5* {25*}

73

222{27*} 5*7*2{46*}1

333{31} 6*13{54*}6*

222{27*} 5*7*2{46*}1

333{31} 6*13{54*}6*

222{27*} 5*7*2{46*}1

3 6 1*{1*4*}6*1

777{75*}7*

3 6 1*{1*4*}6*1

777{75*}7*

3 6 1*{1*4*}6*1

777{75*}7*

3 6 1*{1*4*}6*1

777{75*}7*

2*1* {75*}7*2 6{66*}1 {6*3**}

3{14*} 6* {6*3**}

43{27*} 7*5* {25*}

3{14*} 6* {6*3**}

434{27*} 7*5* {25*}

3{14*} 6* {6*3**}

6*{46*}1 7*{25*}

2*1* {76*}1 6{36*}1 {6*3**}

6*{46*}1 7*{25*}

2*1* {76*}1 6{36*}1 {6*3**}

6*{46*}1 7*{25*}

2*1* {76*}1 6{36*}1 {6*3**}

6*{46*}1 7*{25*}

2*1* {76*}1 6{66*}1 {6*3**}

Married Life Ost Disney UP

{15*}33 {7*5*}33 {6*4*}33　　　　　　{5*3*} 6*7*

{15*}33 {7*5*}33 {6*4*}33　　　　　　{5*3*} 6*7*

131{7*5*}5* 131{6*4*}4*　　　　　　6*16*{5*3**}3**

5*{31}2 6*{36*}12　　　　　　1{6*4*} 5*{6*4*}

121{7*5*}5* 7*27*{6*4*}4*　　　　5*7*5*4* 4*5*4*

3*4*5*{6*4*} 7*{16*} 6*7*{15*}

131{7*5*}5* 131{6*4*}4*　　　　　　6*16*{5*3**}3**

5*{31}2 6*{36*}12　　　　　　1{6*4*} 5*{6*4*}

121{7*5*}5* 7*27*{6*4*}4* 5*7*5*4* 4*5*4*

3*4*5*{6*4*} 7*{16*} 6*7*{15*}

131{7*5*}5* 131{6*4*}4*   136 {75*}7*2

6 {1*6*}17 6   {36*}16 1*{75*}7*25*

1*2*1*{75*}7* 72*7{64*}6*   575{46*} 1 4{36*}1

45 {64*}6* 71*   {1*4*}16 7 {15*}

13{15*}

131{7*5*}5* 131{6*4*}4*   6*16*{5*3**}3**

5*{31}2 6*{36*}12   1{6*4*} 5*{6*4*}

1*2*1*{75*}7*25*   72*7{64*}6*16*

7 5 {1*5*} 13{15*}

Moon River

{55*}1 {2*6*}1 1*

{74*}6*1 654{51}5*

1 {74*}6*1 654{51}5*

1{25*}7*2

3{16*}6* {55*}7* 3

2{16*}6* {56*}1 3

2{14*}6*3 5

{1*6*}13 76{75*}7*2

65{64*}6*136

{55*}1 {2*6*}1 1*

{74*}6*1 654{51}5*

1 {74*}6*1 654{51}5*

1{25*}7*2

3{16*}6* {34*}6*1

5{1*6*} 13 2* 1*{54*}6*1

17654 {55*}7*2

17654 {56*}13

1 {44*}6*2 6* 3{15*}

{55*}1 {2*6*}1 1*

{74*}6*1 654{51}5*

1 {74*}6*1 654{51}5*

1{25*}7*2

3{16*}6* {55*}7* 3

2{16*}6* {56*}1 3

2{14*}6*3 5

{16*}13 76{75*}7*2

65{64*}6*136

{55*}1 {2*6*}1 1*

{74*}6*1 654{51}5*

{74*}6*1 654{51}5*

1{25*}7*2

3{16*}6* {34*}6*1

5{1*6*} 13 2* 1*{54*}6*1

17654 {55*}7*2

17654 {56*}13

1 {44*}6*2 6* 3{15*}

You Raise Me Up

3 {34*}6*2 17*{15*} 5*1

1{25*}7* 116*{5*3**} 1 5*

1{64*}6*1 553{25*}7*5*

7{75*}7*2 654

3 {34*}6*2 17*{15*}

7{75*}7*2 654

7{75*}7*2 654

7{75*}7*2 654

3 {34*}6*2 17*{15*}

1{25*}7* 116*{5*3**} 1 5*

1{64*}6*1 553{25*}7*5*

5*5*1{31} 5*

7*13{51}5*

567 {1*6*}13

{55*}7*2 {31} 5*5 4{36*}1

2 {15*} 5 6 7 {1*6*}13

{55*}7*2 {31} 5*2* 7{1*6*}13

{54*}6*1 5* 57 {1*6*}13

{55*}7*2 {31} 5*5 4{36*}1

5* {15*} 5*5*1{31} 5*

7*13{51}5*

567 {1*6*}13

7{75*}7*2 654	{55*}7*2 {31} 5*5 4{36*}1
3 {34*}6*2 17*{15*}	2 {15*} 5 6 7 {1*6*}13
7{75*}7*2 654	{55*}7*2 {31} 5*2* 7{1*6*}13
7{75*}7*2 654	{54*}6*1 5* 57 {1*6*}13
7{75*}7*2 654	{55*}7*2 {31} 5*5 4{36*}1
3 {34*}6*2 17*{15*}	5* 1 5 6 7 {1*6*}13
7{75*}7*2 654	{55*}7*2 {31} 5*2* 7{1*6*}13
7{75*}7*2 654	{54*}6*1 5* 57 {1*6*}13
7{75*}7*2 654	{55*}7*2 {31} 5*5 4{36*}1
3 {34*}6*2 17*{15*}	5* {15*}

Be Thou My Vision

{15*}1 21 {6*4*} 5* 6*   {14*}6*1 2 {36*}13

{25*}7*2 2 {27*} 3 5   {64*}6*1 53 {55*}7*2

{64***}6*6 7 {1*6*}1 7   6 {54*}6*1 7 {6*4*}4*

{15*} 3 5 {64*}6* 53   13{25*}7* 16*1{15*} 5*

{15*}1 21 {6*4*} 5* 6*   {14*}6*1 2 {36*}13

{25*}7*2 2 {27*} 3 5   {64*}6*1 53 {55*}7*2

{64***}6*6 7 {1*6*}1 7   6 {54*}6*1 7 {6*4*}4*

{15*} 3 5 {64*}6* 53   13{25*}7* 16*1{15*} 5*

{15*}1 21 {6*4*} 5* 6*   {14*}6*1 2 {36*}13

{25*}7*2 2 {27*} 3 5   {64*}6*1 53 {55*}7*2

{64**}6*6 7 {1*6*}1 7   6 {54*}6*1 7 {6*4*}4*

{15*} 3 5 {64*}6* 53   13{25*}7* 16*1{15*} 5*

{15*}1 21 {6*4*}5* 6*   {14*}6*1 2 {36*}13

{25*}7*2 2 {27*} 3 5   {64*}6*1 53 {55*}7*2

{64**}6*6 7 {1*6*}1 7   6 {54*}6*1 7 {6*4*}4*

{15*} 3 5 {64*}6* 53   13{25*}7* 16*1{15*} 5*

{64**}6*6 7 {1*6*}1 7   6 {54*}6*1 7 {6*4*}4*

{15*} 3 5 {64*}6* 53   13{25*}7* 16*1{15*} 5*

True Colors (Phil Collins)

32 11 5*   3455 43 22 31

2 22 321 11 122   3455 55 61

2 22 221 5*1 11   1356 6 5 3 22

1356 6 5 66 66 5   66 55 222 321

1 1 23 1 1 23   3 22 21 6*1

32 11 5*   3455 43 22 31

2 22 321 11 122   3455 55 61

2 22 221 5*1 11   1356 6 5 3 22

1356 6 5 66 66 5   66 55 222 321

1 1 23 1 1 23   3 22 21 6*1

Feelings

{31} {6*3**} 3** 6*

6*7*16* {31} {6*3**} 3**7*6*

6*7*16* {3**6*}1

{25*}7* 5* {7*5*}

{7*5*} 12 {31} 5*

21 {25*}5* 1{7*5*} 5*

{31} {6*3**} 3**7*6*

{31} 22 1 {31}

2{27*} 5* 7* 5*

{31} 22 1 {31}

2{27*} 5* 7* 2

{7*5*} 12 {31} 5*

23{25*}5* 1{7*5*} 5*

{64*}6*136 4*6*1

65434 {55*}7*235 5*7*2

54323 {44*}6*134 4*6*1

{7*5*} 12 {31} 5*

21{7*5*} 5*

{64*}6*136 4*6*1

6 5 4 {55*}7*235 57*2*

5 4 3 {44*}6*134 4*6*1

{7*5*} 12 {31} 5*

21{7*5*} 5*

{31} 22 1 {31}

{31} 221 {31}

{7*5*} 12 {31} 5*

{64*}6*136 4*6*1

54323 {44*}6*134 4*6*1

21{7*5*} 5*

6 5 4 {55*}7*235 57*2*

43*2*12 {31} 5*

{64*}6*136 4*6*1

5 4 3 {44*}6*134 4*6*1

{31} {6*3***} 3***7*6*

2{27*} 5* 7* 5*

2{27*} 5* 7* 2

23{25*}5* 1{7*5*} 5*

65434 {55*}7*235 5*7*2

{7*5*} 12 {31} 5*

{64*}6*136 4*6*1

5 4 3 {44*}6*134 4*6*1

21{7*5*} 5*

6 5 4 {55*}7*235 57*2*

{7*5*} 12 {15*}

Made in the USA
Las Vegas, NV
20 September 2024

95562220R00050